BE FOCUSED, DON'T BE DISTRACTED

ELVIS C. EDOM

authorHOUSE

AuthorHouse™
1663 Liberty Drive
Bloomington, IN 47403
www.authorhouse.com
Phone: 833-262-8899

Published by AuthorHouse 07/14/2020

ISBN: 978-1-7283-6645-6 (sc)
ISBN: 978-1-7283-6644-9 (e)

CONTENTS

DEDICATION

This book is dedicated to the Almighty Yahweh, the creator of the entire universe and all that is in them, whose mercies endureth forever. To my late parents, thank you a million times for having me, also to my siblings, of note Mr. Nnamdi Edom thanks a lot big bro. I will also want to appreciate all those that would make out time to go through this august literary material, you are blessed indeed. My appreciation also go to all my Daddies and Mummies in Yahweh, notably Rev Raphael Egbuna, Prophetess Patience Okeke among others, you are rare gifts to mankind, Yahweh bless you all. May I also use this opportunity to thank all my destiny helpers, those who participated in one way or the other to make this work a great success, and also the publishing team in their effort, may Yahweh bless you all.

FOREWORD

In life nothing destroys dreams and visions like distraction. Overtime, mankind had had to fight in order to overcome this evil, though some succeeded, but to others, the reverse was the case. To those who realized what distraction was and were able to overcome it, the sky was their springboard, but to those who did not succeed, they ended up not leaving much to be remembered for after their exit from this realm, they are regarded as spectators in the world scene, successful people are the real players.

Yes, that marks one remarkable difference between focused successful people and distracted unsuccessful ones. Successful people leave a lot to be remembered for, but that is not the case with distracted ones. For this reason therefore, I thought it wise and imperative that the myth behind focus and distraction should be unraveled.

It is therefore my candid opinion that you would find this material an interesting one indeed, and make a judicious use of the precepts provided herewith. Do have a great day.

INTRODUCTION

There are two key words here, focus and distraction, and these words works in an opposite direction in the life of a man. This is because, in life you are either focused or distracted on your set life objectives. Either way, don't be distracted but rather be focused. These two key words Focus and Distraction shall be the main topic of this discussion.

What then does it mean to be Focused and not Distracted. A look at the origin and the meaning of both words at this point is therefore very important.

The word focus is translated from Latin word "foci" and it means turning attention on areas of concern with the aim of achieving some pre-determined objectives. Distraction on the other hand is also translated from a Latin word "distractio" and it means to pull apart or separating attention on important things. Now let us take it a little bit home, 'foci' or focus as translated is no doubt a very important ingredient needed by every living man to succeed in every sphere of life, be it family, ministry, academic, business etc. But you need to realize that focus and distraction works pari passu, that is to say that as much as you try to be focused in life, distractions are always there for you to deal with. The question then is, what are these distractive elements and agencies and how can they be handled with a view to emerge a champion, living a successful life while on this earth. The answer is not far-fetched, as we progress you will discover that it is still very possible to live through this distractive world and still be focused and achieve your set life objectives.

The greatest tragedy in life is not a failed business, marriage, career etc, but distraction or distractive elements posed by Satan the Devil or his agents that eventually led to those failures. Therefore, it is very imperative for every living being both old and young to be on the alert to guide and pursue their set life objectives. Remember, while alive its pertinent maybe imperative that you achieve your set life objectives, otherwise they remain a pipe-dream because there is no guarantee that your posterity will be able to achieve those dreams, no not the way you want them actualized. Thus, the need to always be focused in life.

The question now is "is it possible to be focused and succeed in a world like ours where distraction is so prevalent? The answer to this question is yes. You also need to realize that many that lived before now were focused and succeeded in their commissions and endeavors despite distractions on their ways on daily basis. A cursory look at some of these individuals will be very helpful at this point in time. Look at the confession of Apostle Paul in (Roman 7:21 KJV "I find then a law, that, when I would do good, evil is present with me.) Did you hear that? Ordinarily, every believer sees Apostle Paul as a successful missionary and evangelist, but in a nut shell, he was just succeeding in the midst of challenges and distractions. Distractions were never a limiting factor to Apostle Paul, he was a super success in his commission, as he affirmed in (2 Timothy 4:7 KJV "I have fought a good fight, I have finished my course, I have kept the faith").What an excellent testimony, this is certainly not a confession of a man that failed due to distraction, and or difficulties. Today we are beneficiaries of his dexterity, going by the number of missions set up by him and the number of Bible books written by him. A focused man indeed you may say.

Master Jesus, our messiah is yet another super success in the midst of distractions and challenges. He was rejected by the people, even though He was telling them the truth, severally, attempts were made to stone him, when He performed miracles, they said He was using the power of Satan. But in the midst of all these He emerged a super success, setting us example to follow as shown in the book of (Hebrews 12:2 (KJV) and it says "Looking at Jesus the author and finisher of our faith, who for the joy that was set before him endured the cross, despising the shame, and is set down at the right hand of the throne of God"). What a man who had his eyes on the prize, no wonder he was never distracted. May I say here that when you have your eyes on the prize, yes, the prize of everlasting life as promised by the Almighty God, you can never be distracted in life? May you never be distracted but, rather be focused as you run this race of life, in Jesus name, Amen.

CHAPTER ONE

The Need To Be Focused

Why do you need to be focused, or "what is the big deal of being focused anyway"? You may ask. In a world like ours where distractions are just around the corner, the need to be focused need not be over emphasized. The bible did not leave us in the dark, in 1 Peter 5:8 (KJV) the bible says "Be sober, be vigilant, because your adversary the devil as a roaring lion walketh about, seeking on whom he may devour". What a warning, a stern one indeed you may say. But that is the real situation we find ourselves today. You need not be told that Satan the Devil and his human agents will go to any length, trying their hands on virtually anything possible to make sure you are distracted, making sure you do not achieve your set life objectives, leaving through this realm a mere spectator. But you would not allow that, would you?

Even the Master Jesus never had it easy while on earth, but he never allowed the cares of this world or the affection of mother, brothers and sisters to affect his works and ministry. In fact He made a complete demarcation between his ministerial duties and family life and welfare, and you too are expected to do so, in Luke 2:49 (KJV) he said" And Jesus said unto them, how is it that ye sought me? Wist ye not that I must be about my Father's business". A serious minded fellow you may say. It is of note that throughout the life and ministry of master Jesus he never allowed anything to come between him and the onerous service He rendered to his heavenly father. He was never distracted, He was focused, in fact He hated even his own life and laid it down that you and I might be saved (Romans 5:8) . And He advised his followers and disciples to emulate his foot-steps. You can read (Luke 14:26, Math 3:32, Mark 10:29,30, Luke 14:26,).Even the affection shown to Jesus by his disciples could not distract him. A look at the account in Matthew 16:23 illustrates this, Jesus had just told his apostles what he would go through in the hands of sinners, and how He would be killed, ordinarily his apostles would not want any such thing to happen to their loving master. Peter now prevailed on Jesus to forbid such things to happen to him, but look at what Jesus had to say (Math 16:23 (KJV) But he turned, and said unto Peter," Get thee behind me, Satan thou art an offence unto me, for thou savourest not the things that be of God, but those that be of men".) A proper look at these words of Jesus is very important;

1) first of all even though he referred to Peter as Satan, he was rather rebuking the Satan that went into Peter to distract him from his pre-determined purpose here on earth. Now you have to realize that Satan is your chief agent of distraction, he would stop at nothing to go into people, things and manipulate events for the sole purpose to distract you. But you have an option to stay focused, unshaken, resolute as a matter of fact. It is not easy as you know, master Jesus was pushed but he resisted, you too can also be tempted but try to resist the antics of Satan and be focused to your life purpose and objectives.

2) Secondly, you need to realize that the Almighty God's purpose for your life might not necessarily please your carnal mind, that is savoring the things of men, God's purpose for your life are spiritual and can only be realized spiritually, such purposes do not please the carnal mind. That is why Jesus said in Math 16:23 (KJV) "for thou savourest not the things that be of God, but those that be of men", showing that Satan is not comfortable with your spiritual advancement and would stop at nothing to distract you, using every weapon at his disposal, especially carnal things. No wonder, the bible say in (Romans 6:8 (KJV) says " for to be carnally minded is death, but to be spiritually minded is life and peace") .Satan has distracted a lot of people by driving them to carnality, they have lost focus to their real life objectives knowingly or unknowingly. So, what is the remedy or what would you do assuming you find yourself in a situation of having lost your focus or distracted. The bible in Jeremiah 6:16 (KJV) says " thus says the Lord, Stand ye in the ways, and see, and ask for the old paths, where is the good ways, and walk therein, and ye shall find rest for your souls. But they said, we will not walk therein". May you never reject or resist to follow the right way when called to order and corrected in Jesus name, Amen. Ask for the old paths, the paths followed by Abraham, Isaac, and Jacob. The path followed by our messiah Jesus. The bible is there to help you, by prayer and fasting, the Holy Spirit is available to help also. There are also men and women taking the lead among us, those called by God, they are there to also help you. It is my prayer today that the help you need to be focused in life, never to be distracted be made available to you in the mighty name of Jesus, Amen. Let faith come to you now, the faith to do exploits, uncommon exploits in this perilous world be made available to you now in Jesus name, Amen.

TO BE FOCUSED IN LIFE, POSITION MATTERS

To be properly focused in life, position matters. So what and where are your positions presently, what are your aspirations, what do you have at hand now to pursue that goal and aspirations? These are some of the very important anticipatory questions that you need to answer in order not to make some unnecessary mistakes occasioned by unwholesome distractions that come in the way of great achievers and goal getters. At this point, answers would be given to the above raised questions in order to get you focused and fully equipped to deal with this issue of distractions.

1) What and where are your positions presently: where you are matters, you need to be at the right place at the right time. You cannot forsake yourself in the gathering of brethren/saints and at the same time you are asking for the gift of the Holy Spirit. If you cannot fast, and deny yourself some carnal pleasures, then you are not just getting it right as far as spiritual gifts are concerned. In fact it means you are distracted by carnal pleasures of this world. You want to grow spiritually, yet you are busy patronizing night parties, night clubs and other indecent places, sorry, but these do not work well with spiritual growth.

Also, if you desire upliftment, growth in the secular world, you need to realize what it takes, for instance you want to be a manager in an oil company. You cannot achieve that with a school certificate in our contemporary world. First, you realize that education is important, years of service and experience, training and retraining that could take quite a number of years cannot be ruled out. Distraction is also not needed. As it is in the secular or corporate world, so it is in spiritual things/world. Need I tell you one axiom? Before you can achieve anything laudable, picture yourself with your mind eyes already having that thing or occupying that position. That is it, don't be distracted, be focused for real.

2) What are your aspirations: what do really want in life. A very good understanding of where you are going will actually make your journey an easy one, that understanding will also help you to be a lot focused in life. A focused man is not easily distracted as you already know. That Mr. A succeeded in telecommunication business, does not mean that you too can succeed there without knowing the skills and strategy involved in that business. Patience is a virtue every success aspiring man must not do away with, it is very important. As you are focused in your aspirations and goals, you also need to back it up with patience. Ask every successful man, and he would tell you how torturous the way to success truly is, it might never be a first attempt thing, so, patience now comes in. Another truth you need to know is jack of all trade is equivalent to mediocrity.

3) What do you have now to pursue that goal and aspiration: some people advices to "cut one's coat according to one's size", but I ask, what happens if you have a large stature but with a lean disposable income, will you still be able to cut that large coat. The answer is in the negative. So, it is in the world of achievers. Many people have very large aspirations, they might be focused as it were, but their financial state will not be able to support or carry them through achieving that aspiration. So, there is a mismatch here, thus, such fellows are now distracted and unable to pursue their goals.

Therefore, I think the right thing is "cut your coat according to the material available". Availability here implies affordability. Go for things you can readily afford, not to stop half way. This is because it is better not to start, than to start and stop half way. Achievers don't stop half way. Drop that idea you may call a white elephant project that is unrealistic, to a lesser but realistic idea that at the end of the day is achievable. For instance, it is a fantastic idea to dream of being a telecommunication giant like MTN (in Nigeria), but you as an individual cannot start up your own business and grow to the size of MTN within a few years, many years of focused hard work and dexterity is highly required indeed. So, what do you have now to pursue your goal? Remember, you might not be the one to actualize the goal you have, sometimes your descendants, the future generations might be the ones to actualize that dream. Take the case of Soichiro Honda, the Japanese inventor of the Honda brand. Soichiro was a teenage bicycle repairer apprentice in his father's workshop in a Japanese remote village, over many decades ago. One day he said "I saw a movable object with noise being driven about in my area, I tried to go closer, but the closer I moved, the farer it goes, at a point I had to run after it, it was so fascinating, so I chased harder after the moving object but my strength was not enough to catch up with it. So, there and then I promised myself that one day I am going to build something like that ". The rest is now history, today we have various brands of Honda automobiles, not necessarily built by Soichiro himself, but he set the stage for what we see today in the Honda world. Certainly, not a distracted man. You too can follow that example, have a dream to be focused to realize it, avoid distractions. It does not matter how long, that dream of yours will still come to pass.

From the above accounts you will see that it is very important to be focused in life, the achievements and exploits of focused people usually out live them as shown by the case of Soichiro Honda, and many other inventors with excellent inventions. Many of them died many years ago, but their exploits are still being enjoyed by mankind today, and will still be here for generations to come. That is to say that focused people live their lives to benefit the entire human race, whereas the distracted live their lives for just their own benefits if at all, but have nothing to offer the human race. So, what choice do want to make now to live through this life without leaving anything to be remembered for or to leave something to be remembered in the annals of history, the choice is yours, and as you do the right thing, the Almighty God will definitely bless you in Jesus name; Amen.

SUMMARY

In this chapter you have learn that:

(1) In a distracted world like ours, it is not easy to be focused. Distractions abounds, even Master Jesus and the apostles had problem with distractions, though they succeeded beyond every reasonable doubts, you too can succeed if only you eschew distractive tendencies and agents. This you can do if only you know what you truly want.

(2) Distraction is something you as a person must have to surmount on your everyday life; you need to be focused on whatever you do in order to overcome it. Even the messiah Jesus was focused, no wonder He was able to fulfill his ministry while here on earth.

(3) To be focused in life, your position do matter, what you are, where you are, your aspiration and what you have at hand to pursue your dream do matter, and is necessary to make you a success story in your world.

(4) You must have what it takes to succeed in your chosen field and career. Be a square peg in a square hole. Mediocrity is not allowed in the world of achievers. Sometime it is needful to get more exposure and education before you venture into that field where uncertainty abounds.

(5) It is good to set the stage for landmark achievements, because when you set the stage, you might not necessarily be the one to actualize that dream. Your descendants and future generations might.

(6) Finally you need the grace of Almighty God and self-discipline to be really focused and distracted in life.

CHAPTER TWO

Is It Possible To Be Focused Now?

Going by the instability in the religious, socio-economic sectors in our contemporary world, this question you realize is not out of place. This is because many today are already distracted without knowing it. They might even think that the situations they found themselves is the will of the Almighty for their life, (what an error) but you need to realize what the bible says in 1 Corinthians 14:33 (KJV) ("For God is not an author of confusion, but of peace, as in all Churches of the saints). You need to realize that if your life and or the condition you find yourself do not give you happiness, then of a certainty, that condition is not the will of the Almighty for you, it takes a focused mind to realize this.

The distraction that come our ways daily have actually made some of us lose focus of our true calling in life. We tend to accept every crumb that come our way as our fair share of the gift of God almighty. Even when they do not come at all, we are still comfortable with that, we may even say we are unlucky, or that the Almighty God do not favor us, thereby giving Satan and his agents enough opportunity to foment more troubles in our lives. Be focused my brethren, look at what the bible says in Jeremiah 29:11 (KJV) ("For I know the thoughts that I think toward you, saith the lord, thoughts of peace, and not of evil, to give you an expected end). The Almighty will not say something in the bible, and do a different thing in our lives. Remember He is not an author of confusion. He cannot lie (Titus 1:2) Be focused enough to realize that that situation you find yourself is not meant to be, neither created by the Almighty to frustrate or limit you in life, but rather the creativity of Satan the Devil and his agents to distract you such that you do not function at your full potential. It is up to you to reject it, seek the intervention of the Almighty God by praying yourself out of that situation. If on the other hand you feel you cannot do it on your own, you can also receive help from the ministers of the Almighty God, through the ministration of the Holy Spirit.

Do not settle for anything less in life, it is the will of your heavenly father that you prosper and make the best out of life. He did it for people in the past, He is still doing it today, and He can also do it for you. The Almighty God is not partial, He is not a respecter of persons (Acts 10:34), He does not look at peoples faces before He favours them. The messiah Jesus once said in Matthew 7:11 (" If you sinful people know how to give good gift to your children, how much more will your heavenly father give good gift to those who ask him" NLT). The Almighty is always willing and well positioned to favour and give good gifts to those desiring and willing to receive from him. The question now is, are you willing? Be focused and avoid distraction in order to receive from him. Though it may not be easy, it was never easy. Nothing good comes easy as you know. But do not allow victimization of Satan and his agents to limit you in life. Say no to his oppression, and mean it. Work and pray assiduously to rebuke him and his antics, fashion out a personal relationship with the Almighty God for a start, and every other thing follows, remember things happens at God's time no your own time. He is the ultimate planner, wait on him, and work with him and you will not be disappointed.

Though, there are factors that can limit you from receiving from your creator, and we shall elucidate them here one after the other;

(1) Living in Sin : sin is a reproach, and everyone desiring to have an excellent relationship with the Almighty God must strive to live above it. Though we cannot deny of being sinful (1 John 1:10), it is not easy to live above sin in a sinful world like ours, but we should show repentance and strive never to go back to sinful ways. The precarious state of this world does not make it easy, the bible in 2 Corinthians 4:8,9 (KJV) says " we are troubled on every side, yet not distressed, we are perplexed, yet not in despair, persecuted, but not forsaken, cast down, but not destroyed ". This is the lot of every child of God on daily basis, but the Almighty God still makes us a way of escape, He never allow us be tempted beyond that we can bear (1 Corinthians 10:13). So, keep the faith and be focused, the Almighty knows our troubles with sinful life that's why He sent his only Begotten to come die for us all (1 Timothy 1:15)

(2) Doubt : the opposite of doubt is faith, the bible admonishes us to do away with doubt but accept faith. In James 1:6-8 (KJV) the bible says " but let him ask in faith, nothing wavering. For he that wavereth is like a wave of the sea driven with the wind and tossed. For let not that man think he shall receive anything of the Lord. A double minded man is unstable in all his ways. What a dangerous thing doubt is. Do away with it today. Hebrew 11:6 (KJV) also condemn doubting and it says "but without faith it is impossible to please him, for he that cometh to God must believe that He is, and that He is the rewarder of them that diligently seek him ". By doubting you already deny beforehand the very existence of the Almighty God, and his wonder working power, a very dangerous thing to do, in fact very disdainful to his personality and, a very dangerous thing to do.

(3) Membership to occult group: the bible in Luke 16:13 (NKJV) says " no servant can serve two masters: for either he will hate the one, and love the other, or else he will hold to the one, and despise the other. Ye cannot serve God and mammon. This is a statement of fact for you cannot serve the Almighty God and at the same time indulge in service to lesser gods. It means you are distracted. You should rather be focused in your service to the only true Living Almighty God, and be sure to receive the full reward. People tend to fear and reverence Satan because of his wicked ways of operation and administration. Matthew 10:28 says we should fear not those that kill the body but cannot destroy the soul, but we should rather fear the Almighty God that can destroy both soul and body in hell. There is no regret in serving the Almighty God, those that served him in the past never regretted, so, you too cannot regret if only you serve him, not in doubting.

(4) Unrighteous living : this factor is rather a subjective one, because the bible says in 1 John 1:8,10 (KJV) " if we say that we have no sin, we deceive ourselves, and the truth is not in us. If we say that we have no sinned, we make him a liar, and his word is not in us ". The bible in Psalm 51:5 (KJV) also says "Behold, I was shapen in iniquity and in sin did my mother conceive me ". Now you see why some would argue that this factor is very subjective. Everything about man from creation is sinful, but that does not excuse man from practicing righteous living to the best of his abilities. By so doing, we attract the ministering angels of the Most High to ourselves, who would in turn reveal some sacred secrets of this life to us. If you may know, the life we live is highly spiritual, and requires a lot of spiritual knowledge to make it a successful one indeed.

So, be focused to understand that this life is not ordinary as some are deceived to believe. It is highly spiritual, but if you live it ordinarily, you end up been a spectator, but if you give it what it requires, avoiding distractions, you end up becoming a champion. The choice is yours, you need to make some serious decisions, and to make those decisions effectively, you have to first ask yourself some heart-searching questions and genuinely provide answers to them. Questions such as (i) what do you really want out of life (ii) what purpose did the Almighty really bring you into this world? These are some of the pertinent question you need to answer, to set off well, and the answers you give to the above questions will jump-start solutions to other life issues you may have.

Nevertheless, effort shall be made here to provide answers to these questions as much as possible to place you on a better pedestal to attend and confront some life issues you may face daily:

(i) What do you really want out of life: this is a very serious question, and effort must be made to define our aim in life in very clear terms as much as possible. Need I say here that some people have turned out spectators here simply because they have not been able to effectively define their aim in life. It is easier to say " I want to be a successful engineer or I want to be a proficient medical doctor" these are all wishes. It does not end there. The ability to turn these wishes into reality is the most important thing. That is to say, the ability to work hard is the most important ingredient required to achieve life aim and purposes. Then, are you ready to work hard and go the extra mile to achieve your pre-defined life dreams and objectives? The answer and choice are entirely yours.

(ii) What purpose did the Almighty bring you into this world: let us go a little bit spiritual this time? Understanding Almighty God's purpose for your life is a very big plus to achieve your life objectives. That brings us to the aspect of destiny. I believe in destiny and it is a very big determinant to what becomes of us in life. Now have you bordered to find out what your destiny is? If your destiny is not to be a wealthy businessman, I tell you no matter how hard you try; at most you will only be a comfortable merchant. In God's arrangement, there are positions for everyone. You can only occupy that He created and made for you. If God has destined you to be a pastor and you are there a lawyer, you can be rest assured that you will hardly succeed there.

So, find out what the Almighty God has destined you to be, and your success story will come like the morning dew.

Nevertheless, your success in life will also depend on your ability to avoid distraction and to a greater extent, how well you are focused.

We shall at this point examine some of the agents of distraction and how to be better equipped to handle them in the next chapter.

SUMMARY

In this chapter, you have learned that:

(1) Many today are distracted without knowing, they accept everything that come their way as the will of almighty God for their lives.

(2) The Almighty God is ever willing to bless us if and only if we are willing to work with Him, He is no respecter of person, His will is what matters most in life.

(3) There are also factors that can limit us and our blessings, such factors are doubting, living in sin, membership of occult group etc.

(4) Life is not ordinary, but many live ordinarily. They end up as spectators. To get the best out of life, give it what it requires through focused and undistracted day to day activities.

(5) To live a purposeful and meaningful life, you need to ask yourself

(i) what do you really want out of life ?

(ii) what is Almighty God's purpose for your life ?

The moment you are able to provide answers to these questions, then you will surely go places.

CHAPTER THREE

AGENTS OF DISTRACTION

The bible in 1 Peter 5:8, says ("Be careful! Watch out for attacks from the Devil, your great enemy. He prowls around like a roaring lion looking for some victim to devour" NLT). Very explicit you may say, but very important here, the bible made us understand here that Satan the Devil is our chief agent of distraction. He distracts us in life using both his human and spiritual agencies, we also as individuals could also be a source of distraction to ourselves. But here we shall be looking at some of the agencies the Devil uses to distract us, and how we can be a form of distraction to ourselves;

(1) Our desires and cares of this world: are yet agents the devil uses to distract us. Master Jesus in Matthew 13:22 (KJV) says ("He also that received the seed among the thorns is He that heareth the word; and the care of this world, and the deceitfulness of riches, choke the word, and He becometh unfruitful"). You can see that sometime our problem is not just about Satan and his agents, but we ourselves. Our inordinate desires and cares, not in tandem with the will of the Almighty God for us are sometimes the source of our problems. Many in their quest to be rich and wealthy have compromised greatly, committing all manner of crime, such as advanced fee fraud, armed banditry, ritual killings, thugs, kidnappings, assassins, to name but a few. In politics and ministerial calling, the story is all the same if not worse. All these evil are done in order to meet up and make quick money, to satisfy the cares of this world as shown in Matthew 13:22. But what is the will of the Almighty God in all these. People tend to have forgotten what the scriptures said in Jeremiah 6:16 (KJV) ("Thus saith the LORD, Stand ye in the ways, and see, and ask for the old paths, where is the good way, and walk therein, and ye shall find rest for your souls. But they said, We will not walk therein" read also Hosea 14:9). The ways of the Almighty God have always been the same; it has never and will not change for anybody. As it was in the beginning, so it is today. The need to walk in the ways of the Almighty God need not be over-emphasized,

the bible says among other things that by doing so, you will find rest for your soul, even though it is said there is no rest in this perilous world, but those that walk in the ways of the almighty God still find rest to their soul. You too can if only you decide to follow him., do not be distracted.

(2) Desires of the flesh and Of the eyes: In Ephesians 2:3 (KJV), the bible says " among whom also we all had our conversation in time past in the lust of our flesh, fulfilling the desires of the flesh and of the mind; and were by nature the children of wrath, even as others". You see, the bible calls those fulfilling desires of the flesh, the children of wrath, what a distraction. I think our desire is to be the children of Almighty God, not of wrath. Many have through their desire to satisfy the flesh lost an excellent relationship they would have had with their creator, very deplorable indeed. All hope is not loss though for those involved, it can still be worked out. A quick turn-around is very necessary from such awkward way of life before it is too late.

It is of note today that sex is one of the cheapest commodities around, and it is advertised in a lot of different ways such as indecent dressing, online nudity and pornography, stripping and naked dances, in fact the list is endless. The streets, offices. Churches, schools, and other sundry places are no longer safe. Sex everywhere, even the universities are not spared. Sex is exchanged for high scores, students prostitution is a norm, for the sake of better living and to meet up.

All these are not the will of the Almighty God for mankind, meaning that people living this way are certainly distracted. The bible in 1 Corinthians 6:19 say "Or don't you know that your body is the temple of the Holy Spirit, who lives in you and was given to you by God? You do not belong to yourself" (NLT, read also 1Peter 2:5). As the bible say, the body being what it is needs no defilement through sexual immorality for those trying to live a focused purposeful life.

Secondly, you also ask yourself what you stand to gain by defiling yourself through sexual immorality, for by practicing such, you will not only offend your creator, you also become vulnerable to numerous sexually transmitted diseases prevalent in the world today. That would not be your portion in Jesus name, Amen. So, be smart, act fast and avoid that avoidable doom.

(3) Inordinate desire for money and material acquisition: the bible in 1 Timothy 6:10 (KJV) says " For the love of money is the root of all kinds of evil. And some people, craving for money, have wandered from the faith and pierced themselves with many sorrows". This is a serious situation, not for a believer desirous of the kingdom.

Please note here that the bible never in any way condemned money, what the bible condemns is the inordinate desire to acquire it as we can see in the world today. Righteous people in the past were known to have acquired wealth. A lot of it and they still served the Almighty God. People like Job as shown in Job chapter one shows that Job was no doubt a wealthy man, yet he led a virtuous life that made the Almighty affirm that there was none like him. People have betrayed their conscience all in an effort to make money, no matter how small or how big. They have the"no holds barred" kind of mentality as far as money is involved. They are ready to go to any length as far as money is involved. Therefore, they are distracted very badly. Job 31:25 says "Does my happiness depend on my wealth and all that I own?"(NLT), a very good question asked there by Job, and the answer is capital NO. Survey shows that a lot of wealthy people are unhappy. Divorce rate among them is very high, some are known to have committed or attempted suicide. Some are on hard drugs, to mention but a few. These are certainly not the attributes of happy people. The bible says in 1 Timothy 6:10 that many in their quest for money have wandered from the faith, and have pierced themselves with many sorrows. Indeed many have derailed; a look at what is going on in many Churches gets you wandering where the leaders and members of those Churches are really headed, all in an effort to increase offerings, tithes and seeds. I am not judging anybody though, but the right thing should be done. Master Jesus in Matthew 16:26 asked " for what is a man profited, if he shall gain the whole world, and loss his own soul? Or what shall a man give in exchange for his soul"? this is what I call the "Irony of riches" and it calls for those pursuing and chasing after wealth to be careful. A word is enough for the wise.

Today kidnapping, armed robbery, prostitution, gigolo, and other forms of social vices are promoted in our society all in an effort to make money. Where does the Almighty God come in, in all these?

Needless, to say that mankind has been greatly distracted from the will of the Almighty God for him in his quest to acquire money and material riches. Very bad you may say, but all these are in tandem to what the bible said in 2 Timothy 3:1,2 and it says " you should also know this, Timothy, that in the last days there will be very difficult times. For people will love only themselves and their money. They will be boastful and proud, scoffing at God, disobedient to their parents, and ungrateful. They will consider nothing sacred " NLT. Is this not what we see in the world today? I know you will sincerely and honestly answer in the affirmative. Assuming you do, what then does it call on your own side, and what line of actions are you now expected to take? To readjust you may say. So, to overcome these perilous times and its consequences, you are to be focused on the word and the will of the Almighty God for your life, and also be focused on the prize, what prize you may ask? The prize of everlasting life in the kingdom of the Almighty God spoken of by Master Jesus himself, (read Matthew 19:29, John 5:24, 6:22, 24, Daniel 12:2).

Do not allow the quest for money to deny you the opportunity of eternal salvation, be focused. Only those that do the will of the Almighty God are sure of their salvation in his kingdom, so, be wise and focused.

(4) The desire to be like others: Youngsters, especially youths tend to be more vulnerable to this particular factor. Nevertheless, full grown adults are not exempted either. That notwithstanding the bible says something in James 4:4 (KJV) "Ye adulterers and adulteresses, know ye not that the friendship of the world is enmity with God? Whosoever therefore will be a friend of the world is the enemy of God". Very startling you may say, but that is the truth. Many unfocused minds today had been led astray due to pressure from close companions. Peer pressure is the worst of all, and this has led youths astray. From the high schools to tertiary institutions, the streets, homes, churches and offices, the story is the same, the wreck wrought by peer pressure in the life of youths. Peer pressures have led many young men to crime such as, armed robbery, kidnapping, drugs gigolo, and many other vices. Young ladies too are not spared either, pressure from peers have left many devastated with unwanted pregnancy, diseases, drugs and other precarious states that can only be remedied by the grace of the Almighty God. Full grown adults, in fact married men and women are not spared of the snare hidden in the desire to be like others. It is of note that some women in their desire to be like and accepted by other women have taken to immoral lifestyle by way of extra marital relationships, in order to meet up high class demand of others. The men also are not exempted. Many good men have turned bad by way of association with evil minded men, some have taken to crime, secret occult groups, womanizing, and several other vices too numerous to mention. But what does the bible say concerning all these? In 1 Corinthians 15:33 (KJV) the bible says "Be not deceived: evil communication corrupt good manners". There is one local adage that says "when an innocent goat forms association with another goat that steals yam, that innocent goat will also form the habit of stealing yam". That is the fact of life. Yam is sweet, even when stolen, it does not matter. That is what peer pressure do in the life of people, it makes you throw caution to the winds, in order to impress and satisfy others, whatever it takes does not matter.

One may ask, are we really living for ourselves, for others or for the Almighty God? Answer to the above question will go a long way in helping solve the problem of peer pressure. If you say you live for yourself, then you are handicapped because you do not have answers to all life issues, neither are you equipped to handle myriads of problem this life presents. If on the other hand you say you live for others, they too have the same problem, if not worse hit than you. You need to realize that some people, who may appear okay, do have problems they hardly share with anyone. They cannot solve their own problems let alone solving your own, so be wise. It is only the true Almighty God you should live for, because among other reasons, He created you, He knows you and any problem you may have. Proverbs 3:5,6 says "trust in the Lord with all your heart; do not depend on your own understanding. Seek his will in all you do, and he will direct your paths" (NLT) read also Isaiah 41:4. You can see even from the scriptures that neither you nor your peers and friends have what it takes to succeed in life, except the Almighty God. So, do not be distracted, be focused and learn to trust in him as the scripture rightly admonished, and all shall be well in Jesus name; Amen

SUMMARY

In this chapter, you have learned that;

(1) Our desires and cares of this world have distracted a lot of us, and care must be taken in order not to get ourselves in messier situation. A line must be drawn between our desires and the will of the Almighty God for our lives. Thereby, we remain focused and not be distracted by our desires.

(2) Sexual immorality has really distracted a lot of people from attaining their desired ends. This agent of distraction has no class, race, ethnic, tribal, religious, social limits. Both old and young are all vulnerable to this agent of distraction. It takes a focused mind to be free from this.

(3) Inordinate desire for money and material things have distracted man and many people have gone astray in our contemporary world today. Many in order to meet up their inordinate financial desires have been into crime and other social vices. They are derailed from the original plan and the will of the God for their lives, knowingly or otherwise. Material acquisition is foremost in the mind of people today rather than the desire to please the Almighty God.

(4) Peoples desire to be liked and accepted by others have actually led them astray from the Almighty God. Many these days are rather interested to keep their friends than having an excellent relationship with their creator. Peer pressure has led people astray, no age limit to this, people wants to be liked and accepted by others no matter what it takes. Not minding how that affects their relationship with God.

CHAPTER FOUR

How Does Almighty God See Distracted People?

Distraction is a recipe for sin and sinful tendencies. Sin is abomination unto the Almighty God; He never permitted nor tolerated it. From the time of the Israelites He never allowed it among his people, in fact sometimes He allowed His heritage, the Israelites to be carried into captivity by invading aliens and be scattered abroad just because of sin and sinful tendencies. Today also, He has not changed, the Almighty cannot work with a distracted person or people just as He never did in the past. Look at the universe for instance, the architectural masterpiece gives credence that its maker and the brain behind its formation was never a distracted mind. The Psalmist was in spirit when He wrote in Psalm 139:14 (KJV), and it says "I will praise thee; for I am fearfully and wonderfully made: marvelous are thy works: and that my soul knoweth right well". Very true indeed, marvelous are the works of the Most High and this is inexcusable. Not only that, the universe with accurate and precise weather, seasons and climate, the human physiology are yet other wonder to behold as we can see and indeed know in every ramification. No wonder then the Psalmist could say that He is fearfully and wonderfully made. Certainly, the wonders of both the universe and the human physiology are not and did not emanate from a distracted and unfocused mind. The Almighty is a serious minded creator who embraces precision in all his creative works and He expects us humans to emulate him. Assuming the Almighty was distracted or in any way unfocused, there are no way these wonders in both the universe and human physiology would have existed ab initio.

Then, the question still remains, how does the Almighty God see distracted people? To help us answer this question better, assuming you as a focused, hardworking man or woman, making effort to survive have an acquaintance or intimately known person who is your direct opposite, what would be your reaction towards him? That also explains Almighty God's reaction towards distracted people. He was and is never receptive of them, because distraction easily leads to sin and sinful tendencies. Take the children of Israel for instance, after their exodus from Egypt, the purpose of the Almighty was to take them to the promise land, a land that flowed with milk and honey. But what happened, while the Most High articulated plans and ideas with his servant Moses on how to settle them in the Promised Land, the Israelites on the other hand were busy molding idols and worshipping them. What a mismatch you may say. They were distracted and carried away from the original plans, arrangements and promises of the Most High who took them out of house bondage with great miracles (read Exodus 32). The consequences was severe and lives were perished because of this singular act from distracted minds, in fact the Most

High was very furious with the perpetrators of this evil such that none of them made it to the promised land, they all died in the wilderness except Caleb and Joshua, only their descendants were eventually the beneficiaries of the promises of the Almighty.

The views of the Almighty towards distracted and unfocused people who eventually derail into sin have not changed even in our time. In fact, today the blessings of the Almighty God cannot be guaranteed for those not focused towards his purpose and pure worship, they might be successful but certainly not blessed. Well I don't want to delve into the difference between a blessed person and a successful person; the scope might be diversionary to the subject matter. The need to be focused in this case need not be over-emphasized, take for instance those in the ministry, if a minister who is called by the Almighty deviates maybe into politics or business enterprises due largely to financial gains, will such a minister still claim to be a torch bearer for the Most High? even though it is very evident he now has divided attention?, you can be rest assured, such an individual cannot do much for the Most High. He cannot carry the much needed fire of the Holy Spirit, even when He succeeds in politics then check his spiritual life. Which shows you cannot serve two masters at the same time, you please one or displease the other (read Matthew 6:24, and Luke 16:13). The Almighty God cannot work with such people.

In the light of the above there are factors that when they begin to manifest in the life of a person then know you are really distracted especially for those in the ministry, and at this point we are going to examine them with a view to be on check and avoid falling victim;

EVIDENCE OF DISTRACTION IN A MAN'S LIFE

(1) Luke warmness in the things that hitherto interests you: this is usually noticed in the life of a man the moment distraction sets in. If the person is usually an early caller to church services, the moment distraction sets, you might find such a person browsing the internet on a service morning, checking for bullish and sheepish stocks in the stock exchange. A very big distraction indeed you may say. And at that point He might even begin to criticize activities of others in the fold, becoming a source of discouragement to others,

whereas the scriptures admonished us to encourage others. He becomes an ultra vires to the fold he belongs, nothing interests him there anymore. At this point rebellion might set in. the fellow at this point is totally out of control and finally disengages by himself or is disfellowshiped by the fold. Sometimes, it should be noted, folks like this usually draw souls away from the truth as they turn out rebels. It should interest you what the bible said in 1 Samuel 15:23a (KJV) "For rebellion is as the sin of witchcraft, and stubbornness is as iniquity and idolatry". It is that bad, distraction can give rise to a whole lot of issues in the life of a man, and the ultimate being that a distracted man loses the favor and approval of the Most High he hitherto enjoyed. He is disapproved at this point and is now a willing tool in the hand of Satan.

That would not be our portion as we guide ourselves against every form of distraction, and have a full focus of the things of the Almighty God. In fact, it is suggested that the moment you begin to notice this factor of Luke warmness or combination of factors that result to it, effort should be made to seek help from a higher spiritual authority like your pastor or other, try your hands on spiritual activities that once elicited a lot of interest and excitement in you. If that does not solve the problem, you might also think of relocating to another congregation or to another Church altogether. All these are undertaken just in an effort to save your spiritual life, and ultimately, to be saved.

(2) Reluctant to pay or avoidance of tithe payment: those who understand the essence of their Christian race do not need a whole sermon to understand and appreciate the importance of tithe payment. Malachi 3:10 is about one of the over-preached bible passage by pastors and evangelists, thereby making Christendom a tithe-conscious faith. It is very evident today that the act of tithe payment and collection has actually been compromised and brought to its lowest ebb in our time. A lot of means and sundry has been devised all in an effort to collect tithe. Sermons upon sermons, some unethical have been preached all in an effort to collect tithe. But, surprisingly, many people still do not pay their tithe. Some have cited the luxurious and ostentatious life style of some pastors as their reason not paying their tithe. They argue, why they would pay from their meager income into the pocket of an already wealthy man. Some even claim they would rather give to the less privileged in the society rather than pay tithe. They see tithe as a task, pastors as task masters. Folks that think and or act these ways are distracted you know. They tend to have forgotten the promises made to people that pay their tithe and the consequences of not doing so (read Malachi 3). It is right to give to the poor no doubt, but that does not take the place of tithe. The Almighty that commanded us to pay our tithe knew the existence of the poor in our midst. Not paying your tithe regardless of who takes it or what its used for, amounts to

disobedient of Almighty God's command, and there are consequences for that. So, pay your tithe, take away prejudice, there are lots of blessings promised and attached to obedience in tithe payment.

Nevertheless, it is still optional to or not pay your tithe, since the decision to do so is entirely yours. And the purpose of this book is not and never to mandate anyone on tithe issues.

(3) Verbal attack, disputes and unnecessary arguments on the things and people of Almighty God: the Almighty God is awesome and his real people, I mean true worshipers are excellently wonderful people. Honesty is one of their significant trappings, just like their father and creator, the Almighty God. Now when a man whom ordinarily should have been a child and worshipper of the Most High turns around to become a thorn in the flesh of children and elects of the Most High, then there is problem. The people of the Almighty God are excitingly charming to be with. They are law abiding loving and generous people, as seen in the past, up till today (read Philippians 4), as they were in the past, so are they today, though there has been a lot of infiltration into the believers fold by mediocre, but the real believers are exemplarily out there for all eyes to see.

So, when a man finds himself at angst against people with the above mentioned exceptional qualities, then such a man is distracted, and a tool in the hand of the evil one, a very bad condition. Given, there might be areas and teachings of a faith and belief that might not go down well with you as a person; this should not necessarily bring about blatant condemnation of the opposing faith. There are rooms for clarification, and that should be fully explored. Under no circumstance should a man's view be seen as inferior without being subjected to the empirical biblical tests and verifications. You know what; everyone has right to their views, whether right or wrong, until empirically and biblically proven. So when you begin to challenge and or attack the things of the Almighty God unwittingly then you are courting trouble.

(4) Disregards and or disrespects to spiritual and constituted authority: this might not interest you but it is necessary. Disregard and disrespect to constituted authority has been the bane of distracted folks. They forget that leaders have civic responsibility to give accurate account on all their subjects. It is therefore very important to respect and obey leaders saddled with such responsibilities. Hebrews 13:17 (NLT) says ("Obey your spiritual leaders and do what they say. Their work is to watch over your souls, and they know they are accountable to God. Give them reason to do this joyfully and not with sorrow. That would certainly not be good for your benefit"). That is the word of the Most High. The Authorities are saddled with the responsibility to shepherd the flocks of the Most High, they are accountable to

him and him alone. Maximum co-operation is demanded from the led in order to make the works of the leaders easy. Also, remember that one day a led could also grow to become a leader, then retribution will set in, for what goes around, also comes around. That would not be your portion in Jesus name, Amen.

(5) Hatred towards brethren and people around: the bible is explicit in its command to us all, that we should love one another, and we cannot afford to do otherwise provided we are still interested to please our heavenly father. It is not optional, we must have to love our brethren whatever it takes, there are no two ways about it, because by so doing we show we are truly interested in the kingdom race. The bible in 1 John 4:7 says "Dear friends, let us continue to love another, for love comes from God. Anyone who loves is born of God and knows God" (NLT) Quite true you know, and the Almighty God exemplified this love by giving his only begotten son to redeem mankind (read John 3:16) hereby showing us how we should love others. The messiah also preached love among his disciples and he said in John 15:12 (KJV) "this is my commandment that ye love another, as I have loved you". This is the word of the Almighty God, and He requires unconditional love for our brethren from us. There are no two ways about it, (read also Hebrews 10:24, 1 Peter 4:8, 1 John 3:11).

Do not be distracted, love is the principal thing in the kingdom race. First of all love for the Almighty will spur us to obey his commandments, and secondly love for our fellow humans, and this will help us not to sin against them. The moment we are able to fulfill these two major obligations, and then it shows we are making progress in our kingdom endeavor. So, be smart to show love to people around you. Do not be distracted thinking you know it all, a professional fault finder. This will do you no good, accept people the way they are, knowing that no one is perfect. Expecting people to live aboveboard is ideal, but in reality no one has any claim to impeccability, that is the reality of life. So, be focused shun excessive criticism and live harmoniously with others and it shall be well.

There are more trait exhibited by distracted people, the wisdom here is not to go through their length and breadth, rather application and amendment of the basic knowledge of the few mentioned will go a long way to make impact in the life of a man. As mentioned earlier, distracted people cannot work with the Almighty, it is not just possible, this is because distracted people are gullible to sin and sinful tendencies. Yes, you can say "but every man is a sinner" as the scriptures rightly said, but a distracted mind will ultimately continue in sin thinking he is on the right tract, in fact he has every claim and facts to justify his actions and inactions. Take the Jewish folks for instance, they have all their reasons to reject the messiah, even when there were prophecies made thousands of years before the birth of the messiah, pointing to where He would be born and events that would surround his birth, but it never mattered to them. Because they were distracted from the truth, such things do not mean anything to them. They persecuted and eventually killed him in a shameful way, believing they were pleasing the Almighty. That is the irony of it all. A distracted man will do the wrong thing and still believe he is on the right track. But that is not the case with a focused man. He is always on the lookout for corrections and ready to adjust no matter what it takes. He does not want to miss out on timely good advice, he is ever ready to make adjustments on areas He feels He is not doing well, that is a focused man for you. So, where do you fall in? A focused or a distracted man? Your honest and sincere answer will go a long way to place you on the right track.

Another integral part of a focused man is what is recorded in Hebrews 8:10 (KJV) and it says "For this is the covenant that I will make with the house of Israel after those days, saith the Lord; I will put my laws into their mind, and write them in their hearts: and I will be to them a God, and they shall be to me a people". That is the most important attribute of a real focused man. The laws of the Almighty God are written on his mind, He cannot do without them, he sleeps, eats, drinks and in fact breaths them. He cannot live outside the laws of his creator; in fact they are his heart beats. He is always looking for ways to please his creator; His delight is in obeying the laws of his creator. What a marvelously awesome life to live, and worthy of emulation indeed. And Psalms 1:2 (KJV) says "But his delight is in the law of the Lord; and in his law doth he meditate day and night". From the fore going, the delight of a focused man is always to obey the laws of his creator. Nothing comes first, or separates him from obeying the laws of his creator. The scriptures say "he meditates on it day and night" it's a way of life for him (obeying Almighty God's laws). One who observes this way of life is already living in heavenly mount Zion, even though he is still here on earth. And he is bound to succeed both in this life and that to come. The race for eternity is utmost in his mind, he is ever ready to obey the laws of the Almighty even at his own peril; Matthew 10:39 says "He that findeth his life shall lose it:and he that loseth his life for my sake shall find it". This is blessed assurance that you can never, I mean never be a loser in Christ Jesus. Even when every other thing is passing away, you remain unshakable. That is just one of the benefits accruable to focused lads. You can see that distractions have nothing good to offer, diminishing returns has always been the lot of distracted folks. So do your utmost to avoid it, in your best interest. No matter where you are now, it is never too late to turn back, pick the pieces and re-launch, starting up your life this time on a focused better pedestal. In addition, you need to realize that distracted people have blind eyes that are why they cannot see what focused minds see. The bible said something about them in 2 Corinthians 4:4 and it says "In whom the god of this world hath blinded the minds of them that believe not,lest the light of the glorious gospel of Christ, who is the image of God, should shine unto them". You can see from the above scriptures that the moment a man is distracted, Satan immediately takes control of his affairs. In contrast to the above scriptures, it is not only the unbelievers whose minds are blinded, there are still those in the faith whose minds are also blinded, and by their fruits they are known. Therefore, one need to be on the watch in order not to fall victim to Satan and his antics. The bible also said something in 1 Corinthians 3:14 and it says "But their minds were blinded for until this day remaineth the same veil untaken away by the reading of the old testament, which veil is done away in Christ". Distraction is a terrible thing in deed, this is because distracted people are not just blind per say, they are actually veiled, such that even while looking they should not see. As pointed out in 1 Corinthians 3:14, "by reading the old testament", which means that these folks actually believe in the Almighty God, but not with the accurate knowledge. This is because any worship of the Most High not based on the ransom sacrifice paid by the Messiah Jesus Christ is inaccurate, and the worshipper is distracted. Now you can see that distraction is a very complicated situation to be in, because, in reality, you may actually be distracted without knowing you are truly distracted.

Now, having come thus far, and equipped with vital materials to handle this ugly situation called distraction, you now have a sense of responsibility to help those in this ugly situation. It might not be easy though, you do not expect it to be, but with genuine persistence, and tolerance you might just be winning a soul back to the fold. You are expected to work for both the Almighty and Humanity in this regards, and a lot of folks out there truly need help, and this material is actually very timely, and ready to use to help bring back the loss to the fold of the Almighty God. You have to put it to good use. A look at Romans 8:19 (KJV) is important and it says "For the earnest expectation of the creature waiteth for the manifestation of the sons of God". This is true and the Almighty expect you to manifest in area of soul winning, and assuming you are saved through the word of the Almighty, you are also expected to save others through the same word you have heard and believed. Sow it also in the minds of others, and populate the kingdom of the most High, and at the same time depopulate the kingdom of darkness, and you would be graciously rewarded for that. I think this word is for someone out there reading this article, "repent today for the kingdom of the Almighty God is at hand". There is no other better time to do that, tomorrow might too late, do that today confess your sins repent from them, confess master Jesus as the savior of your life, the author and finisher of your faith. And all shall be well as you pick your stake and continually follow him, in Jesus name, Amen.

SUMMARY

In this chapter, you have learned that;

(1) The Almighty God from time immemorial had been focused in all his creative activities and as such cannot work with distracted people, in fact He abhors distracted people the same way a serious minded fellow avoids and disapproves a sibling or a friend that is unserious and distracted.

(2) Distraction is recipe for sin and sinful tendencies, this we saw in the life of the Jewish people during the time of Master Jesus, there were prophesies thousands of years before the messiah was born, but because those folks were distracted they refused to recognize him as the one and only true messiah.

(3) A distracted mind is like a veiled bull, even when he is called to order, he throws caution to the wind. He is wrong but he still believes he is doing the right thing. In fact he loathes corrections in their entirety, and will prefer to make all the mistakes rather than being corrected, a very dangerous life to live.

(4) A focused man has the laws of his creator written and inscribed in his mind. He meditates on them day and night, and his steps cannot slip because they are guided in the truth of the most High, even when he falls, he will surely rise again, he hits the ground running. Above all he is blessed above, and beyond measures.

(5) A focused mind just like Master Jesus' is willing to sacrifice everything including his life for the sake of the kingdom. To him eternity is most important rather than temporary enjoyment of sin in this perilous world. As such he is always willing to adjust his ways even when he makes mistakes. None of his actions is rubber stamped; he is ever flexible directed by the eternal truth as contained in God's word the bible.

(6) As a focused mind, walking in the light of the truth from God's word the bible, you are saved to save others. You are encouraged to help others with what you have learned from this material, remember the commission given by Master Jesus in Matthew 28:20, to increase and populate the kingdom of the Most High and to decrease and depopulate the kingdom of darkness, Halleluiah.

CHAPTER FIVE

BENEFITS OF BEING FOCUSED IN TODAY'S WORLD

The benefits of being focused in life need not be over-emphasized, the same way you do not tell a pedestrian on a busy high way to be watchful before crossing the road. In fact, in everyday life it is even more expedient to be focused and careful because we live in a perilous world, at a time the bible calls the last days. The bible in the book of 2 Timothy 3:1 (KJV) says "This know also: that in the last days perilous times shall come". Yes, the bible already forewarned believers about the nature of the time we live in, and you know to be forewarned is to be forearmed. Going by the words of the Almighty God as evidenced in the bible every believing child of the Most High should not be oblivious of what is happening in the world today. But for those who are focused nothing come to them as a surprise, because the bible has already prophesied about them, so they would surely come to pass, for it takes a focused mind to know that every prophecy foretold by the Most High will surly come to fulfillment. This is one of the benefits of being focused in today's world. If you go further in the book of 2 Timothy 3:2-5 (KJV), the bible says "For men shall be lovers of their own selves, covetous, boasters, proud, blasphemers, disobedient to parents, unthankful, unholy, without natural affection, trucebreakers, false accusers, incontinent, fierce, despisers of those who are good. Traitors, heady, high minded lovers of pleasure more than lovers of God. Having a form of godliness, but denying the power thereof: from such turn away". You can see what the bible said about the last days and from what we see in the world today, you will no doubt agree with me that it is here with us, so, care must be taken by every focused mind, because all the signs are here with us already. Indeed, the last days are truly here, no doubt about that.

Another benefit of being focused in the light of all these is that we are not taken unawares in the scheme of things, as the signs unfolds, we will know that they have already been foretold, and it would not be strange to us, though we do not know the actual day and time, even the messiah also did not know while here on earth, we are not also taken unawares (read Mark 13:32 and Matthew 24:36). But like the five wise virgins as spoken of by the messiah himself in the book of Matthew 25:1-13, we need to be vigilant, up and doing at all time in order not to lose our chances of salvation.

Nevertheless, the grace of the Most High is also needed at all times for the bible says in the book of Acts 15:11 (KJV), and it says "But we believe that through the grace of the Lord Jesus Christ we shall be saved, even as they". The bible still goes further in Ephesians 2:5,8 (KJV)to say "Even when we were dead in sins, hath quickened us together with Christ, (by grace ye are saved). For by grace are ye saved through faith; and that not of yourselves: it is the gift of God". Furthermore, the book of 2 Timothy 1:9 (KJV) says "Who hath saved us, and called us with an holy calling, not according to our works, but according to his own purpose and grace, which was given us in Christ Jesus before the world began". You see, it is not all about good works, righteousness that we are saved, but every focused person should also ask for the grace of God in order to be saved. To give credence to the above axiom, the condemned man alongside the messiah on the tree of Calvary received salvation right there at the point of condemnation because grace was at work, if not what good works and righteousness would a condemned criminal who may have committed a lot killings and robbery be associated with, to attract salvation to him. In fact I see grace as the most important ingredients for our salvation, because the bible describes our righteousness as filthy rags before the Most High God himself. The book of Isaiah 64:6 says "But we all as unclean thing, and all our righteousness are as filthy rags and we all do fade as a leaf; and our iniquities, like the wind has taken us away". The above is the exact state of every man, but by his grace, we are renewed and made fit for his salvation. Therefore, every focused man ought to in addition to his good works and righteousness, also ask for grace to be saved.

Another benefit of being focused in today's world is that we are guided to add strength to the process of evangelism. Soul winning as pointed out earlier in this book is the heart beat of the kingdom race. Every focused mind is expected to par-take in this, for by so doing the bible says "you will save yourself and those who listen to you". 1 Timothy 4:16 says "keep a close watch on yourself and on your teaching. Stay true to what is right, and God will save you and those who hear you". From the above scripture, you can see that the act of soul-winning is purely a divine appointment and our salvation is also dependent on it. Our Messiah himself in the book of Matthew 28:19,20 (KJV) commanded us and said "Go ye therefore, and teach all nations, baptizing them in the name of the Father, and of the Son, and of the Holy Spirit. Teaching them to observe all things whatsoever I have commanded you; and, lo, I am with you always, even unto the end of the world. Amen". Now, let us observe the above command very critically;

(1) First of all, you can see that the command is coming from the Messiah himself and must be obeyed if only we want to show ourselves truly as obedient servants. Remember this command is not only meant for pastors and evangelists only as some are distracted to believe, it is actually for all believers, Christendom in general. We are expected to evangelize in season and out of season that is in favorable and unfavorable condition tell people around

you what the Almighty God has done in your life, in fact, the life you live is a very big miracle, you can start with that. In addendum, we as Christians are supposed to be soul winners at all times. You need not be timid or ashamed while doing this, remember your life and peoples' lives are involved. (Read 2 Timothy 2:15)

(2) Secondly, as we obey this command in Matthew 28:20, the Messiah promised us of his protection. So we need not be timid or fearful in carrying out this onerous divine service or worried about what to speak when we come face to face with a potential convert, or when faced with persecution, the Messiah said in Matthew 10:19 (KJV) "But when they deliver you up, take no thought how or what ye shall speak for it shall be given you in that same hour what ye shall speak. You might cite insecurity and or persecution as your reason for not speaking up, but not to worry all that have been taken care of. You can go about it informally; yes informal preaching has worked out in uncertain conditions, exactly what the messiah did with Samaritan woman in the John 4:10, 11. The overall aim is to pass your message across no matter what, and as you do, you will be richly blessed.

(3) Finally, you can see that this command is a continuous exercise till when the Messiah comes. Do not tire out or discouraged. Be courageous and faithfully continue in your commission, for the reward is enormous, in fact beyond your imagination. Just keep faith and be focused, for those that will obey, be instant about it for the time is now. The bible in Matthew 24:44-50 (KJV) says "Therefore, be ye also ready: for in such an hour as ye think not the son of man cometh. Who then is the faithful and wise servant, whom his master has made ruler over his household, to give them meat in due season? Blessed is that servant, whom his master when he cometh shall find so doing. Verily, I say unto you, That he shall make him ruler over all his goods. But and if that evil servant shall say in his heart, my master delayeth his coming; and shall begin to smite his fellow servants, and to eat and drink with the drunken; the master of that servant will come in a day he looketh not for him, and in an hour he is not aware of, and shall cut him asunder, and appoint him his portion with the hypocrites: there shall be weeping and gnashing of teeth.

In conclusion, for focused people, soul winning is very expedient in this end time, and the time is now, nevertheless, you are expected to receive the word personally and allow it sink down and make desirable changes in you first, before you go about preaching to others. Otherwise you might end up being hypocritical.

From the above, you can see that one of the most important benefits of being focused in this end time is that you will be doing the will of your father which is in heaven, and by so doing, you become a subject of his heavenly kingdom by way of salvation of your soul. So, what would you be doing? For the time is now and the choice is yours to quickly readjust your ways and arrest your passions that are not in tandem with the will of the Almighty God.

Another important reason of being focused in life is that focused people are happy people; they are not carried away by illusion created by daily worldly events. In fact when they see certain events taking place in our daily life, they are quickly reminded about bible prophecies foretold long time ago, and how it is been fulfilled in their time, then instead of being saddened by such events they are rather encouraged to keep the faith because they have just witnessed the fulfillment of yet a prophesy long foretold, by so doing they are once again reminded that the time is closer than they ordinarily thought. What a happy moment that would be to a focused believer who is abreast with time. The everyday people take worldly event literarily, but that is not the case with an expectant, focused believer of the word. Prophetic events of our time do not pass him by, they are indeed very remarkable to him, he finds his place in the fulfillment of those events. He is not a bystander. He is conscious and takes his place in the fulfillment of bible prophecies.

A focused mind have nothing to do with failure, unlike the distracted people who see failure as part of the game of life, a focused mind cannot afford to fail in the duties commissioned to him by his creator. Failure to him looks like the end of the world, for to such a fellow it will mean the kingdom of darkness have triumphed over the kingdom of the Most High God, (Abomination) you may say, but that's how he sees it, and will work pro-efficiently hard to ensure such scenario do not prevail.

A focused believer is pragmatically realist, he sees things as they appear, has no place for ideals and abstractions. Note that abstraction is the hallmark of distraction, and a whole lot of folk's daily dwell on this. He is ready to work with anyone, even the worst sinner with the aim that the sinner would be won for the Master at the end of the day. He is ready to make sacrifice for the kingdom race, and the Almighty is the winner at the end of the day. He does not expect everybody to meet his standards, neither does he expect everyone to be perfect realizing that he as a person is not perfect. Kingdom race is uppermost in his mind, and soul winning is his priority.

A focused believer does not procrastinate; he realizes that procrastination is the worst destroyer of time and opportunity. He takes and works with every opportunity as they present themselves. He does not postpone events as they come. He works with every event as they come with the mindset to get the best out of them. As pointed out earlier, he is less conscious of failure. He has the "can do" approach to life events. To him, there is no time to try again later, and he is result oriented.

Focused people are super humans. When you are focused in life, you conquer the world of impossibilities. To you, nothing is impossible; there is no barrier to your world of achievements, and at this point the bible book of Job 22:29 (KJV) becomes true to your life, and it says "When men are cast down, then thou shall say, there is lifting up; and he shall save the humble person". That means when and where other people fail, you go there and succeed. In fact, people desirous of success will come borrow ideas from you; you become the giver of good ideas. At this point, everybody will want to be your friend because they know the benefits they stand to derive by associating with you, you become a true charismatic fellow. All these are allude to focused individual, because when once you are focused in life, success becomes your next name, and everybody like to be associated with success and successful people.

So, having seen the benefits of being focused in life, it is my belief that you would aspire to be counted among folks who succeeded in their earthly endeavors because they were wise and focused enough to their various callings.

SUMMARY

In this chapter, you have learned that;

(1) It takes a focused mind to know that the period we live in is actually that prophesied by the word of the Most High as the last days, as recorded in 2 Timothy 3:1-5. Therefore, one is not taken unawares by the turn of events as they unfolds, knowing fully well that these have already been foretold.

(2) More than ever before, understanding the time we live in, we are encouraged to be proactive in telling others to turn away from their evil ways, assuming we have already made amends in our own ways of life, because by so doing, we would save ourselves and those that listens to us.1 Timothy 4:16 says "keep a close watch on yourself and on your teaching. Stay true to what is right, and God will save you and those who hear you". Act on this for it is very timely.

(3) In whatsoever state we find ourselves, we should always ask for the GRACE of the Most High, for we are not saved by our righteous living. In fact, the bible makes it clear that our righteousness is like filthy rags before the Most High God. So, grace speaks better on our behalf than our righteousness.

(4) A focused man like his creator has no place in his life for failure. To him it is a win/win situation. Always willing to set up good foundation and work towards a better goal. He is always willing to give good attention to all his endeavors, and good results follows suit.

(5) Being focused makes you become pragmatic in your dealings. At this point, you are not willing to cut corners, as a realist you see things as they are, you don't blame others for your mistakes and misfortunes. But willing to make amends when there is need to procrastinate.

(6) A focused man does not procrastinate. He takes every opportunity and makes excellent use of them acting as if they would never come again. He does not postpone events. He always wants to get the best out of every event.

(7) To a focused man, the world of impossibilities is a fallacy. He is an achiever regardless of the circumstances surrounding him at any point in time; he goes all the way to get what he wants, no matter the obstacles on his way.

(8) Finally considering the ways and achievements of a focused man, he leaves a legacy behind him and his life is truly worthy of emulation.

CHAPTER SIX

THE MOMENT OF TRUTH

It is my candid believe that thus far you have had a lot of mind re-orientation while reading this material, if you did, then that is very splendid indeed. On the other hand if you are yet to fully come to terms with the life changing truths as contained in this material, then you still have the opportunity to benefit from the light of truth as evidently portrayed in this august, soul-enlightening literary material. For this is the moment of truth, from here, we shall be examining our stand, where we truly are and be able to know from our stand if we are focused or otherwise, distracted based on what we know so far. The bible in 2 Corinthians 13:5 (KJV) say "Examine yourselves, whether ye be in the faith; prove your own selves. Know ye not your own selves, how that Jesus Christ is in you, except ye be reprobates"?, How timely, self-examinations is very important in the kingdom race, and also in the contemporary daily life. This is because there has been a lot of compromise in the societal norms, things that hitherto constituted affronts, today is accepted as normal way of life. Some have even justified the abnormalities in the society to mean modernity and new trends. But the bible has no place for modernity, because the bible standards do not and will never change as far as the Almighty is concerned, He changeth not, as He was in the beginning so He is today, and so He would always be (read Psalm 15:4). So, you already know that as a focused child of the Almighty there are things you ought to do, and there are things you are not supposed to do base on bible standards and principles. Even though such things have become the societal norms, the bible discourages them and you as a believing child of the most High God are encouraged to abstain from such evil practices. Now examine yourself, in this moment of truth, you are expected to tell yourself the one and only truth, are you sure that as a focused mind you are following these timely truths? This is a personal question that requires personal answer, for it is between you and your creator.

Based on 2 Corinthians 13:5 (quoted above) the author of this material is also daily asking himself these questions, if not more. If you may know the laws of the most High is meant to be obey by all, no matter how highly or lowly placed we might be in the society. Having said that, the yard stick every believer uses to judge or examine himself as the bible said above is the ten commandment of the Almighty God. Remember the Almighty God is no respecter of person, his standards and laws are sacrosanct and must be obeyed (the Ten Commandments). Remember that the Ten Commandments is designed to expose evil to highest level, with no exception, and must be obeyed in totality, and not in isolation. James 2:10 says "And person who keeps all of the laws except one is as guilty as a person who has broken all of God's laws" (NLT). So, you can see the seriousness of the matter, self-examination, it needs all the attention it deserves, and to get it right you need to sit down and properly study the bible, get proper explanations where you are confused (read Roman 10:14). The moment you get the accurate knowledge from the bible, the next step is to ask for grace that the Almighty God alone can give, in order not to make mistakes. At this point you now have a bible-trained conscience, very important for everyday life.

At this point your speeches and actions are guided by the bible truth. Before you act or speak on any subject matter, you will want to know what the bible says about it. You become a kingdom subject, conscious of the heavenly race. That might not be the end of the matter as various temptations will surely come your way, but with the help of the Almighty God and prayerfully, you will surely overcome. Let faith come to you now and it is the will of the most High God that you will overcome every obstructions on your way, in Jesus name, Amen.

That is not yet the end of the matter, as continuous self-appraisal is very necessary (2 Corinthians 13:5), you need to be honest to yourself as to how good or how badly you have fared, the bible in 2 Timothy 3:14 (KJV) says "But continue thou in the things which thou hast learned and hast been assured of, knowing of whom thou hast learned them". This is very important as you continue to regularly run through the word of the Almighty, with time, it becomes part and parcel of you. At this point you can hardly do without it. Hardly will you stay a whole day without reading your bible, not just reading it but practicing what you read. At this point;

(1) your mind is renewed, Romans 12:2 (KJV) says "And be not conformed to this world: but be ye transformed by the renewing of your mind, that ye may prove what is that good, and acceptable, and perfect, will of God". A renewed mind is a repented mind and it's a mind destined for salvation. Though, mind-renewal processes are not as easy as they sound, they are in fact frothed with pit and falls. That is why you see a fellow who claims repented still going back to sin, it is a process full of trials and care must be taken not to be judgmental of people struggling with this process. Nevertheless, the moment mind renewal processes is effectively completed, it is so marvelous that you see worst sinner becoming saint. And it is my prayer today that those who seek to have their minds renewed will find grace to do so in Jesus name, Amen.

(2) You become a new creature, Romans 8:1 (KJV) says "There is therefore now no condemnation to them which are in Christ Jesus, who walk not after the flesh, but after the Spirit". Yes, a new creature is a creature that has overcome the old, sinful self. He is no longer the way He used to be. The new creature is a creature liberated from the old strangulating hold of Satan the Devil and sin. As it goes there is no condemnation to that soul, every fear and guilt of sin has been done away with as far as this fellow is concerned. The law of his creator is upper most in his mind, and pleasing his creator is something he cannot trade with, not even with the purest gold. Above all, He is sure of his salvation.

(3) people around you will begin to testify that you are truly a changed person a repented child of most High God, Matthew 5:16 says, "Let your light so shine before men, that they may see your good works and glorify your father which is in heaven"Halleluiah, It is said that "there is no hiding place for a golden fish" a renewed, recreated child of the Most High is such. He always finds a pride of place in the will of his creator. The Most High will do nothing without first of all revealing it to him by way of dreams and or visions. He is important in the sequence and events of spiritual things. People of good cheers are always attracted to him, because there is a lot to learn and gained from him. Please, brace up and work hard to attain that level and status, for there will be no regrets and disappointments by so doing, praise the Lord.

As mentioned earlier, continuous self-appraisal is very important to attain this level of spiritual equilibrium where you fall in line with the will of the Most High for your life, nonetheless, you are also expected to carry others along as you grow in line of spiritual things. The bible in Matthew 28:19a says "Therefore, go and make disciples of all nations, (NLT). Very apt and straight as command from the messiah himself, you are expected to participate in this august service to humanity, remember lives are involved, need I tell you that soul winning is the heart-beat of the kingdom race, no wonder apostle Paul in 1 Corinthians 9:16 (KJV) declared "For though I preach the gospel, I have nothing to glory of: for necessity is laid upon me, yea, woe is unto me, if I preach not the gospel". Now you have seen what the scripture say, so take a decision to partake in the preaching and teaching aspect of soul winning and as you do the Almighty will surely bless you.

Having seen above the attributes that marks a man out for reckoning, take a decision today to factor yourself in, in this divine arrangement for by so doing you have a lot to gain.

But I also need to remind you as mentioned earlier that the process of mind-renewal is not an easy one, for you have to brace up for a lot challenges that come with it, persecution might come from places and people you least expect. Family members and trusted friends might even be sources of biggest challenges. Do not be discouraged or disappointed when some of these traits begin to manifest, remember the path you have decided to take is rather a divine instruction, and necessity is laid upon you to carry on with it, the bible in Acts 5:29 (KJV) says "Then Peter and the other Apostles answered and said, we ought to obey God rather than men". Yes it is of immense benefit to obey the Almighty in all things no matter the consequences, those who did in the past never regretted, you too would never regret as you do in Jesus name, Amen.

SUMMARY

In this chapter, you have learned the following;

(1) That in the kingdom race there is need to continuous examine ourselves through the bible standards to know truly if we are still in line with the will of the Most High for our lives.

(2) That the process of mind renewal is very important for every kingdom conscious child of the Most High. This is very important to make us the new man that the bible expects us to be before we can be sure of our salvation.

(3) The moment our mind is renewed, we become new creature and people around us will now begin to testify that we are truly changed person, and this change manifests in every areas of our everyday life. At this point, we become light of the world, and source of encouragement to others, especially the unbelievers.

(4) That continuous self-appraisal is very important in the process of mind renewal, because we need to know how well or how badly we have fared over time.

(5) That this process is not an easy one, it is prone with pits and falls because persecution can also arise even from close friends and relations.

(6) Soul winning is important for believers; you are saved to save others. Preach the word in season and out of season, in favorable and unfavorable conditions. (See Matthew 28:19).

(7) That in every situation, you are expected to obey the Almighty God rather than men, even while faced with family or peer pressure. This is because at the end of the day, every man will carry his own load and answerable for his own deeds and misdeeds.

CHAPTER SEVEN

So What Do I Do Now?

This is a personal anticipatory question that needs an urgent answer in order to be placed on a better pedestal in life, now and that to come. To effectively provide an answer to this question, let us look at what the bible says in Ecclesiastes 12:13, 14 (KJV) and it says "Let us hear the conclusion of the whole matter: fear God, and keep his commandment: for this is the whole duty of man. For God will bring every work into judgment, with every secret thing, whether it be good, or whether it be evil". Did you see that? In fact obeying the commandment of the Almighty is an integral part of worshipping him. In order words, you cannot claim you worship the Almighty God if you do not keep his commandments. Bearing in mind that every work, and the kind of life we live while here on earth will surely come to judgment at the end of the day should rather spur us to live the right kind of life based on the bible principles, there are no excuses here for every work will definitely come to judgment, whether good or bad. We are therefore, expected to worship our creator very selflessly no matter our circumstances. No wonder the bible says that the Almighty created man to honor and worship him and him alone. Let me bring it home as to what you are expected to do, from the context of our discussion thus far;

(1) You are expected to make a total turn-around from any way you led your life that does not glorify your creator.
(2) Total change of attitude is also expected of you based on bible principles.
(3) You also need to make strong decision never to go back to your old ways of life that does not glorify the Almighty God.
(4) Finally, you ask for the grace to remain steadfast in your new found faith/ way of life.

We will now take time to examine each of these steps and see what they entail in the decision making process of an average believer;

(1) As stated above, among the decision processes, to have a right standing with the Almighty, you are expected to make a total turn-around from your old ways that do not bring glory to the Most High. I will liken this process to a man travelling in the high way to a particular destination. But suddenly, he discovers that he is on a wrong direction and there is need to change direction. Would he now say because he has covered a long distance to a wrong direction, so he would not turn-around? Funny as that may sound, but that is true irony of life, and many find themselves in this situation, for it is never too late to make adjustments in life provided you know what you are doing and where you are going. In this context, you are expected to be armed with right knowledge as provided in the bible in order to make this decision very effectively. Total turn-around from ways that do not bring honor and glory to the Almighty is very crucial for those desirous to succeed in the kingdom race.

(2) You also need total change of attitude in your quest to make it to eternity. Yes at this point you will need to find the word of the Almighty and the things of the Almighty very interesting. Nothing comes first in your preferences. At this point, the word of the Most High becomes food to your soul to such an extent you cannot do without it. You can hardly spend a whole day without reading the bible; in fact it becomes a way of life. Maybe before such was not the case, but it's no longer the case at this point because there has been change of attitude.

It may not be easy though, to adjust to new ways because temptations will always come your way, look at this confession of Apostle Paul in Romans 7:15 (KJV), and it says "For that which I do I allow not: for what I would, that do I not; but what I hate, that do I". This is true because the wrong things are more pleasurable to do than the right one, and this makes the kingdom race a very difficult one. Nevertheless, the bible consoles us with these words; Matthew 10:22b (KJV) says "but he that endureth to the end shall be saved".

(3) You see temptations would come, but you really need to make strong decisions never to go back to your old ways. Like the book of Matthew 10:22b quoted above shows the travails of every believer, but you must make decision to endure temptations, as they come, persevere in faith and your will to do the right thing . As mentioned earlier, it is not easy to adapt to all these, but the Almighty knows our struggles and our desires to do the right thing, and He would surely provide us with ways, and strength to succeed.

(4) The grace aspect is the most important aspect in the process to live right for the Almighty, this is because many people often make decision to live right and make changes in their ways of life, only to go back in no time to their old ways, and might even get worse than they were before they hitherto took decision to change their ways. This is because grace is not at work. For in an atmosphere of grace, the Devil and his demons are on the run. No

wonder the Messiah admonished his disciples to always watch and pray, in Luke 21:36 the bible says "Watch ye therefore and pray always, that ye may be accounted worthy to escape all these things that shall come to pass and to stand before the son of man". The messiah here was actually telling his disciples to ask for grace to run the race of life and never to backslide, and they did and were graced, to persevere in faith even under strongest of trials. The result? They emerged champions; you too can if only you are willing. So, are you willing? Your answer should be personal.

Having said this much, it is my candid believe that you would use what you have learn to further your life the more as a focused man, nevertheless, if a different image crops up on your mind telling you a different thing other than what you have been made to believe, please reject it in its entirety, that is not the voice nor the will of the Most High for your life. Rather, focus on the things that are consistent with the words of the Most High God concerning you.

It is therefore my candid belief that you have learn some things and maybe, been reminded of some other ones while reading this material, now you have the opportunity to take all you have learned with you, and start to work with them. For by so doing, you will no doubt live a glorious and victorious life that the Almighty God has reserved for you from creation, remain Blessed.

SUMMARY

In this chapter, you have learn the following;

(1) That to be focused in life, your ultimate guide will be to obey the laws of the Almighty creator, for that is the whole duty of every living man. Nevertheless, by so doing you will exhibit the sterling qualities of the creator himself, who is not known to fail in his various endeavors, that is you will end up being like him in all that you do.

(2) That it is never too late to make adjustments in life provided, you actually know what you want and where you are going. There are always rooms for adjustment for every living man, death is the only end of it all, for even the thief with the messiah on the torture stake still had the opportunity for salvation.

(3) That to turn to new ways is froth with temptations, but we are encouraged to persevere in faith because it is only those that endure to the end that will be saved.

(4) That above all, to succeed in life, you need the grace of the Almighty to make good every decision you have so far taken. Without grace working on your side, chances are you might still go back to your old ways or even get worse than you were before you made decisions to make changes. The Messiah knew that, that's why He admonished his disciples to always watch and pray.

(5) To utilize all that you have learn from this material and make a decision. Forfeit and reject any voice or messages from the evil one that leads you to do anything contrary to the will of the Most High for your life as contained in the bible, and as prescribed by this material. Such messages are not useful in any way, you should focus on the things and ways of the Most High, they are sure ways to success and salvation.

ABOUT THE AUTHOR

Bro Elvis C. Edom (B.Sc. Finance and Banking) is the founder of Graceworld Outreach, a non-denominational gospel evangelical body. A multi-talented preacher and teacher of the gospel, as a prolific writer, he has also contributed, coauthored many books and tracts, among which "reach out to the water of life, the life giving water", which is being distributed and circulated nationwide.

Bro Elvis is also an accomplished technocrat, having worked in oil servicing, and maritime logistics companies (a loss-control specialist), rising over time to the rank of senior manager. Presently, for the love of the things of the Almighty, he has dedicated his life to do the will of the Most High by way of the preaching and teaching work, hope you would find him interesting.

Printed in the United States
By Bookmasters